GET PAID TO DO
What You Love!

DESIGNING THE CAREER & THE LIFE
THAT YOU'VE ALWAYS WANTED

By

JANET GREENWALD
&
LAURA GREENWALD

Published by Stuf Productions/Lion and the Rock Entertainment

For information about special discounts and bulk purchases go to www.getyourstufftogether.com or email corpsales@getyourstufftogether.com.

Manufactured in the United States of America

ISBN: 978-1533410078

Table Of Contents

Chapter One

PUTTING THE PURPOSE BACK INTO YOUR CAREER

Putting the Purpose Back Into Your Career

Imagine having a career that matches your personality and desires so closely, that it would be hard to believe you were put on earth to do anything else. The kind of job that makes you jump out of bed on Monday morning ready to take on the world. Wherever you go, you radiate dedication, excitement and love for your work. That sparkle in your eyes tells the whole story.

People like that are just fortunate, you say. They knew somebody or were in the right place at the right time. But most of the time, those happy, passionate people didn't fall into their careers. They just always knew what they wanted to do as if they had an onboard compass showing them the way. If they got off track, they just re-evaluated, figured out where they were supposed to be going and got right back on.

But most people don't have this kind of internal directional system with bells that go off the moment we lose track of our purpose. Or do we? How many times have you said, "If I could only open my own business, I'd be happy." Or, "Someday I'll go back to art school and finish that degree."

What makes some people dream and others do? We're thoroughly convinced that it's all a matter of taking the time to find the purpose of your life. Not _in_ your life, _of_ your life. We're not talking philosophy, just creating a perfect blend of your interests, natural talents, your needs, wants and desires.

When people are truly focused and passionate, really believe in what they're going after, that's when they succeed. And that's what makes the difference.

What Is *Get Paid To Do What You Love?*

Get Paid To Do What You Love is a program of guided exercises designed to help you realize your inborn talents and dreams. Our main goal is to bring to the surface the person you originally were before school, family and society got a hold of you and molded you into what they wanted you to be.

Once you rediscover your original dreams and abilities, this book will show you how to turn those dreams into reality with a new career, business or a new focus for your life's work. After all, they're your dreams, so the way you decide to use them, is entirely up to you!

Get Paid To Do What You Love is not a career counseling guide. It wasn't designed to test your aptitude or job skills or to tell you specifically where you fit into the job market. It won't tell you how to write a resume or how to interview. There are already hundreds of terrific books that can help you with that.

So why did we write this one? We did it to fill the needs of people who are stuck in a career or lifestyle that is completely wrong for them and need to find their way back to their first love.

We're a mother and daughter writing team, who has had our share of jobs and careers. Some were wonderful, like our first jobs in production working with actors and producers on the sets of prime time sitcoms. And others? Don't even ask! And right in between are the jobs that, whether you mean for them to or not, turn into careers.

What we've found is that the people who take the time to examine what they like to do, what they're good at and then design a career to match their skills and desires, usually end up happier, more fulfilled and more prosperous than their peers. You're going to spend forty to sixty hours a week, fifty-two weeks a year for thirty or forty years working at some kind of a job. Wouldn't it be wonderful to have a career you loved? Want to see something startling? Do the math. Forty hours a week, fifty-two weeks a year for forty years. That's eighty-three thousand, two hundred hours!

We were watching an interview with actor Jim Carrey one time and the interviewer asked him point blank why he's still working so hard, making one movie after another. After all, as he said himself, he's made so much money, he'll never have to work another day in his life. As he thought about it, this wonderful glow came over that animated face and he said, "Because I love to tell stories. I love what I do so much that I can never imagine retiring, no matter how much money I have."

Wow! Can you imagine what the world would be like if everyone loved his or her job THAT much? I'm happy to say that we can! And so can millions of other people.

Not only was that one of the most important goals for our lives, but it's also the reason we wrote this workbook. We wanted to design a simple, straightforward book to help you put that kind of love and passion into every one of those 83,200 hours.

What Do You Love To Do?

Over the next several pages, you're going to do exercises that were designed to examine six different areas of your life. They'll help you figure out two things: what you love to do and how you can make money doing it. Sound simple? Maybe, but then again universal laws usually are!

One word before you begin. This isn't the kind of workbook that you can score and find out what someone else thinks you should do with the rest of your life. The only expert analyzing these questions is you. Just do each of the exercises and put your answers to the side until we're ready to start sorting them out. So with no further ado, let's get started!

Chapter Two

LET'S PLAY A GAME

Let's Play A Game

Do you remember the park you used to go to when you were little? How about the playground in your elementary school, the forts and tree houses you built or that cozy corner of your room? Remember when you could be a firefighter one minute and get elected president the next?

When we were kids, playing was our job. It's how we learned about the world, our friends and ourselves. As we experimented we tried on different roles, adopting or rejecting them as we found out what we liked and what we were good at. This is usually the earliest glimmer of life's purpose.

Remember when you could be or do anything just by using your imagination? That's what this exercise is all about. Grab your #2 pencil. Ready?

EXERCISE 1

Think back to when you were three or four years old. If you have trouble remembering that far back, dig out some old photos or call your brother and sister or mom or dad, to see if they can spark some memories. Try to picture your first clear memories of childhood.

A. What toys did you like to play with? What games did you enjoy? Did you like to play with others or alone? When you were alone and allowed to do whatever you wanted, what did you do? What made you happy?

B. How did you approach things? Were you detail oriented or did you just jump in and have fun? Did you make big projects for yourself or did you enjoy simple things? Did you build things or tear things apart to examine them? Did you make your own fun or want to be entertained?

C. As you got older and joined more organized groups or sports, were you a leader or a follower? Did you like school? What did you excel at? Do poorly in? What did you do during your preteen and teen years when you were alone? Did you develop any hobbies or interests that were important to you?

Chapter Three

DO YOUR DREAMS MATCH YOUR LIFE?

Do Your Dreams Match Your Life?

We were all put here for a purpose.

Think about that for a moment. Can you imagine a world where everyone is doing the job he is best suited for? Workers would actually be happy and fulfilled. And, because they would be good at their jobs, they'd get more promotions and better pay. If you think they'd be happy, imagine their supervisors, managing productive, well-trained employees. Okay so it's idealistic, but wouldn't it be great?

There's a place in all of our hearts that safeguards a very special gift, which I believe is given to all of us the instant we're born. Everyone's gift is different, tailored to his or her unique talents, skills and environment. What is the gift? Your desires.

The word "desire" literally means "of the Father". Since the word comes from the Latin, let's see what the Bible says about it. Hmm, here's an interesting verse. "Delight in the Lord and He will give you the desires of your heart." Go back and re-read that sentence very carefully. Not only does it say God will grant your desires, it says that He's the one who gives them to you in the first place! That means that everything you've instinctively wanted to do all your life, the jobs you always "knew" you'd be good at, all the things you love to do, to be around, all those good and positive things, are God-given.

Examining your dreams and desires can give you clues to that purpose. Once we start walking towards our real desires, doors open and give us an opportunity to test the new waters. And the best part is, all we're really doing is stretching the muscles that are already there.

EXERCISE 2

A. What did you want to be when you grew up, when you were in elementary school? High school? College?

What did you fantasize that your life would be like? Did any of your childhood dreams come true? If so, how did it happen? Is this a part of your career today and if not, do you want it to be?

16.

B. The first time you were seriously considering a career, what did you want to do with your life? What intrigued you? Why? Did you tell anyone? Did they encourage you? Discourage you?

Did anyone encourage you to follow their dreams instead of your own? Did you do what you set out to do? Did it make you happy?

EXERCISE 3

It's time to do some daydreaming. No, not about a deserted island and a buff, perfectly-tanned native. This dream is about a day in your ideal life and there's only one rule. Everything you write about must be something you seriously want. Otherwise you have our permission to be absolutely outrageous. Have fun with it!

Now let's begin. It's a few years into your future and you're well into what you want to be doing.

So, tell us about it. Write everything in the first person. Look around. What are your surroundings like? What kind of people are you with? Take a careful look at every area of your ideal life.

Do you live in a large house instead of your loft? Are you working for a large corporation, a small one, or do you work from home? Detail is absolutely crucial, so write every bit of it down.

What do you look like? What types of clothes are you wearing?   Who do you work with? What types of people are they? Do they work with you or for you?

.

What do you work on during the day? How many hours do you work? What gives you a sense of accomplishment in this ideal world?

Now let's kick that picture into 3D. Close your eyes and look at that image of that job or business again. What colors are you wearing in the image? What color is the room you're in? Is it bright or dark?   Adjust the image; make it lighter and darker, change the colors, play with it until you get a mix of colors and images that really excites you and describe the changes you've made below.

Close your eyes and take another look at that image, but this time, turn up the sound. What sounds are surrounding you? Is it busy or quiet? Are you relaxed and comfortable or excited and filled with energy? Is your family there, your friends, co-workers? How are they interacting with you? Make this scene, so real that you can touch it, feel it, see it anytime you want. Capture it in as many vivid details as you can in the space below.

Chapter Four

YOUR LIFE SO FAR...

Your Life So Far...

I bet you knew this was coming. This is the section where you examine all the jobs, education and outside activities you have ever had. So grab all your old resumes...

EXERCISE 4

List every job you have ever held. First write the job title and then write down every part of the job that you enjoyed. As much as you may have disliked a job there is almost always something you can find that you liked. Don't forget to include volunteer work and internships. If you run out of space use another sheet of paper.

1.

2.

3.

26.

4.

5.

What were your favorite subjects in high school? What fascinated you? What did you study or read about even when it wasn't assigned to you. What about college and graduate school? List all of those subjects below.

In the career or job you have now, do you have the opportunity to use what you learned about that subject?   For instance if you loved English Composition, does your career give you the chance to write?   If you were a science buff, do you have the opportunity to explore new concepts and problem-solve on the job?

Circle the three subjects that you loved the most and write down ways that you can make these interests a part of your everyday life.

Finally, write a list of outside interests and hobbies that you enjoy. What is it that you enjoy the most about each one? Is it something you would like to make a career out of or integrate into your life? If so, note ways that you can see yourself doing that.

Chapter Five

RECAPTURING THE DREAM

Recapturing the Dream

PART ONE

In this section, you'll begin to design your career and your life. Yes, design. Most of us take more care making sure our towels match than deciding how to spend our lives. So let's get busy. What you're going to do now is put together all the exercises you've done so far. Exercise #4 comes first.

In the first part of this exercise, you listed the things you enjoyed doing at work. Read over them again and choose the top six or seven areas that you want to use in your new career. Write them down below.

Now take a moment to look over Exercise #1. You probably have quite a few answers that uncover some of your earliest interests and abilities. Which ones still intrigue you or excite you? If you still want any of these things to be a part of your life, write them in below.

EXERCISE 5

We're going to turn all this information into a statement. We want you to put each interest, ability or desire in a sentence, then weave all the sentences into a statement describing yourself. And don't use job titles. That's the way the world categorizes people – we're trying to think out of the box! For instance, instead of "I like being an accountant," say "I enjoy working with numbers," or "I'm good at keeping organized ledgers".

Finished? It's time to take out the Dream section homework, Exercises 2 and 3. Take a moment to read over your daydream. If you want to add or change anything, go ahead. We forgot to mention this but all exercises are subject to revision!

Read over Exercise #2. Did you discover any dreams that have gone unfulfilled? Is there anything the exercise revealed that you would now like to pursue? What do you absolutely love to do? What would you do even if you weren't paid to do it? Try to work these things into your ideal daydream.

Get the dream as perfect as you can. Use as many pieces of paper that you need to use. Remember, during this ideal day, anything is possible.

Focus entirely on yourself and how you want to feel, what you want do and how you interact with others, in your daydream. The more detail the better. If you can't put a name to the job you want to be doing, that's all right. Just focus on the things you want to be doing during your day.

I realize that writing about the past brings up a lot of memories. It might have made you feel extremely accomplished or might have brought up a lot of unhappiness and pain. Whatever surfaced, take a moment to be proud of what you've done so far. You've done the best you could, working in a less than perfect system with people who aren't always out for your best interests. But the important thing is, you're here and you're ready to begin the next, most exciting chapter of your life!

One more thing before we go on. I want you to take a moment to give yourself permission to be everything that you want to be. No doubts, no "yeah but...". It's already yours. Just have a little faith, step out, and take it.

Now let's go make it happen.

Chapter Six

DESIGNING YOUR CAREER

Designing Your Career

By now, you probably have a good idea where your purpose lies. It will fall into one of two categories -- a career path you will follow while working for someone else, or striking out on your own to start a business. The steps needed to make these dreams a reality are a bit different, so for this chapter, we're going to deal with the people who will be designing a career, where they'll be working in someone else's company.

Read over your daydream once more and realistically compare it to your present career. How different is it? You can use a separate piece of paper if you'd like or just jot down a few of your thoughts below. What skills are you going to be using in your new career? How many of them do you already have? Imagine for a moment that you are in the office of your prospective employer, interviewing for the job you want. What skills and training would you want to be able to tell the employer you possess, in order to clinch that job?

Now turn it around. You're the employer. What would you want to hear from this person to convince you that she can handle this job?

All right, now imagine you've aced the interview and now the human resources person wants to see your resume.

EXERCISE 6

Have you ever wanted to create an absolutely perfect resume – one that includes all the experience you don't have, but know you need to snag the career you want? Well here's your chance! Before you begin this worksheet, stop to think about your target career. How soon do you expect to be ready to step into that job? Weeks, months, years? Consider where you are now, the skills and experience you already have and what you will have had to accomplish to land that job, by the time of the interview. Be honest. If you need extra training or a few more years of experience, say so. Being brutally honest with yourself will give you a much better chance of landing your new career.

JOB DESCRIPTION

Describe the job you want in detail, what you'll do all day long, the skills that you'll need to have, the kind of person you want supervising you, the kind of people you'll be working with and the type of customers you'll be dealing with.

EXPERIENCE YOU ALREADY HAVE

Even if it's not in the same field, how will your past experience help you in this new position?

EXPERIENCE YOU'LL NEED TO GAIN

Don't forget to tell us how you propose to get it.

WHAT PROFESSIONAL ORGANIZATIONS SHOULD YOU JOIN

Also note which ones might be able to help you find the position you want.

CONTACTS

Do you know anyone who already has a job like this? Someone who already works in this field? Identify at least ten people, whether you know them personally or not, who can help you with your career change.

OTHER INFORMATION

Why do you think that you can do this particular job? And you'd better make it convincing. You're writing this for a pretty tough customer – you! Until you convince yourself that this is the job for you, you'll have a hard time convincing anyone else.

Chapter Seven

BUSINESS ANYONE?

Business Anyone?

You want to start your own business? Fantastic!! Instead of simply presenting a resume, and letting the personnel department do its thing, you're going to have to convince someone else of your ability to establish a business and make it flourish. If you have a certain business in mind and certain skills that you want to be using, how many of them do you already have? How can you get the rest?

Let's say that you want to open your own antique shop. You can just see the grand opening, a champagne reception taking place amid the emerald green and mahogany walls. Flowers everywhere. But, wait a minute, you have no experience in store management and your antique expertise is limited to browsing. It won't be impossible to open a shop, you just need a plan. A business plan.

Picture yourself across the desk from your friendly local bank's loan officer. His face has gone from sunny to grim as you hand him his fifth business plan of the morning. Change places with him for a moment. What would you want to see on that plan? Write a few notes on the type of business you're opening. Does your background fit in with the experience you'll need to make a go of it? What skills and experience would the owner of this business need to be successful? The next exercise is in the form of a business plan. With that dour faced loan officer in mind, write this plan as if you already have all the skills, training and contacts you'll need to make him approve your loan.

EXERCISE 7

Have you ever wanted to create an absolutely perfect business plan – one that includes all the experience you don't have, but know you need to open that business and make it successful? Well here's your chance! Before you begin this worksheet, stop to think about your business. In fact, close your eyes for a moment and step into your shop or the main office of your business. Watch yourself successfully dealing with your customers and employees.   How soon do you expect to be ready to open shop? Weeks, months, years? Consider where you are now, what skills and experience you already have and what you will have had to accomplish to be a huge success!

If you need extra training or a few more years of experience, say so. Being brutally honest with yourself will give you a much better chance of getting that business off the ground.

BUSINESS DESCRIPTION

Describe the business you want to create in detail, what you'll do all day long, the skills that someone already in this business would have to have, the kind of people you'll be working with and the type of people that your business will help or serve.

TARGET MARKET/LOCATION:

EXPERIENCE YOU ALREADY HAVE

Even if it's not in the same field, how will your past experience help you in this new business?

EXPERIENCE YOU'LL NEED TO GAIN

Don't forget to note how you'll get it.

PROFESSIONAL TRAINING & SKILLS

Things that will help you build your business, like sales training, bookkeeping experience or highly specialized training in your particular area of business.

WHAT PROFESSIONAL ORGANIZATIONS SHOULD YOU JOIN

And write down which ones might be able to help you create and build your business and customer base.

CONTACTS

Do you know anyone who already has a similar business? Someone who already works in this field? Identify at least ten people, whether you know them personally or not, who can help you create your business.

OTHER INFORMATION

Why do you think that you can open this kind of a business? And you'd better make it convincing. You're writing this for a pretty tough customer – you! Until you convince yourself that this is the business for you, you'll have a hard time convincing anyone else.

Chapter Eight

TURNING YOUR DREAMS
INTO GOALS

Turning Your Dreams Into Goals

Now you know what you'll need to make your dream a reality. Is your goal reachable? If you're sixty years old and have never taken a singing lesson, chances are you'll never be featured soloist at the Met. That doesn't mean that you can't take lessons and entertain as a hobby. Make a list of everything you'll need to do to make your real life resume or business plan match the one you just created. Then break each large goal into smaller, more manageable steps and finally assign a date to each one.

GOAL #1 - I will do:

By this date:

My first step is:

My second step is:

My third step is:

GOAL #2 - I will do:

By this date:

My first step is:

My second step is:

My third step is:

GOAL #3 - I will do:

By this date:

My first step is:

My second step is:

My third step is:

GOAL #4 - I will do:

By this date:

My first step is:

My second step is:

My third step is:

GOAL #5 - I will do:

By this date:

My first step is:

My second step is:

My third step is:

Chapter Nine

ACHIEVING THE DREAM

Achieving The Dream

You have your dream and your present life laid out in front of you, and you understand the rudiments of creating the future you want. Now comes the actual work of getting that dream.

There are many useful tools in getting your plans off the ground. I'm going to briefly mention a few of them. Although some will be more effective for certain situations, they can all be useful to you.

Targeting Transferrable Skills

Using Exercise #4 and your old resumes, look for skills that you have gained on other jobs, in volunteer work, internships, or simply through life experience, that can transfer to your new career. For instance, let's say that you want to become a copywriter in an advertising agency and that last fall you wrote brochures for your local chapter of the American Heart Association. Whether the brochure you wrote was for a charity fund raiser or a major corporation makes no difference, it's still advertising and copywriting experience.

If you have trouble thinking about your unpaid or non-workplace experience as real work experience, think again. Companies all over the world are looking for people who can make a difference, who can get the job done and achieve measurable results, regardless of stellar job titles or extraordinary salaries. When the choice comes down to hiring you or a twenty-two year old who doesn't have a clue how to deal with people, or real situations in the real world, you'll get the job. That is, if you're able to communicate your real world abilities in a way that your future employer can understand.

No matter what your experience, corporate or volunteer, take a few moments to go back over Exercise #4 and write the results you accomplished in each job or position you listed. No job titles here, just specific measurable results. An achievement like, "Oversaw the marketing and rollout of the new fall line of widgets, resulting in a thirty percent increase over previous year's sales", will fit either a Microsoft marketing executive or someone who makes and sells her own jewelry.

Or how about, "Supervised a staff of ten people, as they worked to create branch offices of the organization out into new areas and recruit workers to run them". Are we talking about a bank or the regional head of the Boy Scouts? See what we mean? Absolutely true, absolutely valid experience communicated in the language of whatever career or business you're targeting. Experience is experience and your prospective employers want to know what you've done for others and what you can do for them.

Create Your Own Resume -- Revisited

You've identified the skills you'll need to fulfill your purpose. But how do you get them? One way is through your present job. Is there a job or a department that's similar your target career or business? Or what about volunteering for a committee, or talking your boss into sending you to a relevant seminar or training program. Better yet, find a way to quietly incorporate these new skills into your daily routine at work. As your proficiency grows, your co-workers and your boss will accept them as if they'd always been part of your job description. Make sure to document your new experience on your present resume, as you begin to get it under your belt.

If your present job is just too limited, look to community service or charities for the experience you need. Ask if you can fill a volunteer spot doing what you want to learn. Or you might even get to work with someone who is already a local expert at the job you'll soon be looking for. Either way, you'll be giving a charity the help they need and they'll be giving you the experience you need. Talk about a win-win situation!

O.P.E.

You've heard of O.P.M. right? It's a great piece of advice that always comes up when someone is buying a house or opening his own business. The advice? Whatever you do, don't tie up your own money, use **O**ther **P**eople's **M**oney. We're going to take that a step further. There are two ways to learn anything in life. You can either start from scratch and emerge a few years later well-educated but bruised and bloody from being knocked through the ropes. Or you can find other people who have already accomplished what you're setting out to do, and use the knowledge they've gained to meet your goal faster, easier and with a lot less bruising.

O.P.E. - **O**ther **P**eople's **E**xperience! While you're researching your new career, you'll probably come across people who are already doing what you want to do, or you can find them on LinkedIn. Don't be afraid to contact them. Most people who are passionate about their work will be happy to answer questions and give you advice. This is a great way to make contacts and learn about your field. Nancy Anderson has written a wonderful book called "Work With Passion" that outlines an entire job-finding method based on using advice calls.

Your friends are another excellent source of information. You probably have a friend or two who are doing a job similar to the one you want or who have opened a business like the one you want. As long as you're not going to be a direct competitor, take them out to lunch and pick their brain for a while. Or if they run a business, ask them if they could use a volunteer during a busy season. One thing that we've learned is that most successful people love to help! They just never get the chance, because no one ever asks them. What a waste of a wonderful resource. For an in depth look at O.P.E. in action, check out *Get Paid To Do What You* Love In Action, later in this book.

Training Programs And Internships

You don't have to be in college or freshly graduated to take advantage of training programs. If you find the perfect program to bridge the gap in your skills, ignore the requirements. Call the administrator, make an appointment and explain your special circumstances. Don't be shy about telling them what someone of your experience can bring to their program, as well as what it will do for you. When the two of us were starting out in television production, we found the perfect internship at a major production company in Los Angeles. Everything should have been against us. Here we were a mother and a daughter. Not only didn't we have college degrees, we had almost no TV experience and we were relatives for goodness sake!

Even so, we walked into the HR department of a company that at the time was one of the largest providers of sitcoms and dramas. We immediately we saw a room full of applicants for the same internships we were after, all fresh out of film school. We looked at each other and asked the receptionist who was in charge of internships. She gave us his name and extension, so we picked up a courtesy phone and called him. He listened as we told him why we were there and the background we had. An hour later, we had the last two internships, right on the stage working with the actors, crew and producers.

Chapter Ten

TELL ME WHAT YOU WANT IN ONE PARAGRAPH OR LESS

Tell Me What You Want
In One Paragraph Or Less

Nothing in this world is more important than communication. You can have the best experience in the world, but if you can't communicate that fact to the person holding the purse strings, you're out of luck!

Letter Writing 101

Why a section on writing letters? In this increasingly text/email/tweet friendly world, people are losing their ability to communicate through writing. Yet, when you're trying to land a new job, that's one skill you desperately need. Think about it. Most job openings request a resume with a cover letter. So does LinkedIn by the way and you'll always get a better response to a connection request if you write an actual note to the person you're targeting. And, if you decide to use the advice call approach, you'll want to contact people with a perfectly executed letter. A letter, especially a cover letter, is your representative. It's there to explain your resume, describe you to the employer and persuade them to call you in for an interview.

So how do you make one little letter do all this work? First, figure out what you want the letter to accomplish. If you're responding to a classified ad, you obviously want to secure an interview. Now look at the ad carefully. What qualifications do they need for the job? Which of those skills do you possess? Make some notes. This is your chance to explain why you think they should hire you. Now read between the lines. What kind of person do they want? Good personality? Organized? Analytical? Jot down all the adjectives you feel would describe the perfect candidate. As you begin to write the first draft, slant the descriptions of your experience towards these adjectives.

When you write the first draft, forget about spelling and grammar, just get your ideas down as quickly as possible, then go back and build your thoughts into paragraphs. Start with a statement. What job are you applying for? Then describe your experience as it pertains to the position. Tell them why you want the job and what you, as an individual, can bring to it. Finally, ask for a meeting.

If you're writing to someone in a field that is new to you to set up an advice meeting, the letter will take a little more thought. Who is this person? What do they do? What makes them so good at their job? Why do you admire them? Tell them. A heartfelt compliment is always welcome. Why do you want to meet with them? What do you hope to accomplish from the meeting? Be specific, be sincere, and be brief, but most of all, make sure that this letter represents you in the way you want to be seen.

The thing we want to emphasize is, you don't always have to follow the rules. If you have a different slant on something, don't assume they'll say no, ask. Maybe no one has ever thought of it before. Even if they do turn you down, you'll know you tried. You and you alone are responsible for creating your life's purpose and executing that purpose any way you can.

E-Mailing Your Way To Success

Technology is a wonderful thing and it can go a long way toward helping you find and create your perfect career. Only a few years ago, people and information were very difficult to find. Now between the Internet and e-mail nearly everyone and everything is accessible at the click of a mouse.

In the entertainment industry usually the personal approach works best. For example, as writers when we're trying to pitch a movie or television series idea, the best person to speak with is either the head of a production company or (a more likely scenario), their director of development. Whether you have an agent or not, these people are busy and it's always good to be able to grab their attention. I'm happy to say that we've found a great solution that works in almost any field. Go ahead and write your advice call letter as detailed above. But add two simple yet extremely effective steps.

First do a little research on this person. There is usually some background information on most people of local or national reputation, on the Internet. You're looking for anything you might have in common with this person, that you can touch on in the letter. We also like to see if we can find anything that the person has written her or himself, which always provides a little insight into the way they talk, what's important to them, even the way they think.

It's fun if you make a game of it. See what kind of language they use. Do they use visual words – "I see, it appears, take a look"? How about auditory words – "I hear you, that sounds about right to me", or vivid rhythms and words you can practically hear, like "tolling" or "thunderous"?

Or do they use kinesthetic words – "It feels right to me, they sense," or words that connote touch and sensation? Whatever kind of words they use the most, means that this is probably their dominant sense, the one they use primarily in communication. Then look over your own letter and see if you change some of your own words to include words from their dominant sense. Don't laugh, it helps foster a feeling of comfort, that you two speak the same language. You'll already seem like someone they'll enjoy talking with.

Second e-mail your advice letter to them. Most people open their own e-mail from their own computer, reducing the chance that your letter will be confiscated by a well-meaning assistant. For major corporations, e-mail addresses are usually pretty easy to find, either by calling the company to ask the e-mail address of the person you're writing or by looking at the company's web site.

Usually companies use the same format for all of their employee's e-mail ie. firstname.lastname@widget.com or firstinitiallastname@widget.com, you get the idea. Just look for the e-mail address of other employees at the firm on their web site. One good place to start is their media contact page or a list of sales people. They almost always will have an email address for at least one person. Then use the same format for the person you want to reach. And if you can't find it that way, try typing *.*@companywebsite.com, substituting the url of the company you're trying to reach. That usually brings up a few email addresses, so that you can follow the format.

The best part about emailing your advice letter, is that it works! Not only do we know immediately that they've gotten our letter and that it's waiting for them right where they live – on their desktop – but we've gotten extremely positive responses from nearly everyone we've e-mailed.

Chapter Eleven

GET PAID TO DO WHAT YOU LOVE
IN ACTION

Get Paid To Do What You Love in Action

The Choice Of A Lifetime

You can read hundreds of books, go to seminars, answer questions until your eyes glaze over and set extraordinary, life-altering goals, but unless you do one thing, none of that will make a bit of difference. You have to make the choice to change. You are the only one who can decide to take your life in a different direction and then perform all the changes necessary to do it. It's all a matter of choice.

In order to make the changes necessary to follow the road map you've designed for yourself in this program, you're going to have to make a decision. The decision to change direction and follow your new path. In the Latin, the word "decision" means "to turn away from". When you make the decision to change your life, you are literally deciding to turn away from all of the old ways of doing things that produced those old results and old situations you're trying to get rid of. Does that make sense? There's a great quote attributed to Alcoholics Anonymous. "The definition of insanity is doing the same thing over and over again and expecting different results." In order to get new results, whether that's your new career or new path for your life, you're going to have to do things in a different way.

The Most Powerful Word In The Universe

We're fans of that great success coach and motivational speaker Tony Robbins. There's one piece of advice he gives that we'd been doing long before we ever heard his CDs and using it produces absolutely magical results. In his CDs he builds the suspense to an absolute crescendo by saying that doing this one thing will get you whatever you want in life. He makes his students take out their notebooks and get ready to write for hours on end to capture all the nuances of his advice. Pencils ready? There's one sure way to get absolutely anything you want in life and it all comes down to the most powerful word in the universe.

"ASK".

When you want something or need something – advice, brainstorming, a personal contact – whatever it is, find someone who can give it to you and ask for it. It's that simple and it moves mountains. Case in point. A few years ago a personal situation took us out of our normal careers as writers and propelled us headlong into the world of politics. You already know we're a mother and daughter team. Well, when our mother/grandmother died at the hands of a Chicago hospital a few years ago, our grief at her sudden death quickly turned to outrage when we found out that she'd actually been hospitalized for seven days, not a day and a half as we'd been told.

You see, the hospital "forgot" to call us and Grandma, a vital, wonderful seventy-one year old woman, died alone. We didn't even know she'd been hurt from a fall at home, let alone that she was dying. Long story short, while researching the case, we discovered that only 4 out of 50 states have laws stating that hospitals must notify a patient's next of kin, even if the patient is unconscious or unable to physically give informed consent. Armed only with an idea and the text of the next of kin laws from those few states, we set out to change that. Our goal was to enact a next of kin law in California (where we live) and Illinois (where it happened).

Impossible? Probably. Daunting? You bet! But if you have a big enough "why" in your life then it's pretty easy to come up with a "how" – a game plan. And this time we had one. Right in the pages of this book.

Chapter Twelve

Building Your Own Personal
Advisory Board

Building Your Own Personal Advisory Board

Talk about being your own guinea pigs!

I'll tell you one thing, we learned more about setting achievable goals, asking for what we needed, recruiting mentors and building our own advisory board in one year than we'd ever learned in our lives. Of course we already had a huge advantage, just like you do. We've gone through all the exercises in this book and know where our skills and passions lie. For example we know that we both have strong writing, research and PR skills, that we have a lot of media contacts and have always been fascinated with the inner workings of politics. By the same token, we also knew our weaknesses and it only took a few days to figure out the kind of advice and help we'd need to make this happen. Did it work? We'll let's just say that not only do California and Illinois now have next of kin laws, but every one of the votes for the Illinois Bill (five to be exact) were absolutely unanimous. The beauty of this system is that it will work whether you're creating a new job for yourself, building a business or lobbying the state legislature.

Here's a quick breakdown of the action system we used with the legislature.

1. Identify what you need.
2. Ask for it.
3. Recruit mentors
4. Build your own advisory board

Identify What You Need

Except for sophomore civics class and watching every episode of "The West Wing", neither of us had a day's experience in politics. So after discovering the fact that there were no laws regarding notifying a patient's family, we did what any good writer would do. We researched the subject to pieces! Which told us what kind of law we needed, but not a thing about how to write one. As we said earlier, there are two ways to learn anything, getting knocked through the ropes or using the knowledge of someone who's already been there. We opted for door number two.

Once we had the text – a mixture of the best features from each of the states who had NOK laws – we decided that we needed to know two things: 1. Who to take our legislative idea to, and 2. How to get it enacted.

Ask

We began by asking those two questions of everyone we could find who had anything to do with enacting similar laws in California and Illinois, or healthcare legislation in general. Early on, we got a great piece of advice from the head of a university who's known for getting impossible things done in record time, by thinking completely out of the box.

What he told us was terrifying and flies in the face of conventional logic. It also worked. He told us to get in touch with everyone who we thought would be opposed to our bill, present the idea to them and ask them for their help in writing a version of it that they would feel comfortable backing.

So we looked for the California legislator who would be the most opposed to a bill that would impose regulations on doctors and hospitals even in an emergency situation. We found one, a Senator who not only had a medical background, but had a husband who is a doctor and had also enacted tons of important healthcare legislation. She loved the bill and she and her staff worked with us to make it patient, hospital and doctor friendly without diluting it. There's no sense enacting a bill without the teeth it needs to make it effective.

Even though she wasn't the Senator who ended up carrying the bill, without her input, we probably never would have been able to get it through those first channels. Every time we spoke to someone we asked them for the names of organizations or people that they thought would either have a say in enacting our bill, or be opposed to it.   Because we asked the right questions, we ended up working with hospital, medical and nursing associations, even the state healthcare authorities to hammer out the text.

And just like the head of the university predicted, these were precisely the people who the legislators turned to, in deciding whether or not to vote for our bill. Imagine their opinion of our bill when they found out that those associations not only were backing it, but had a hand in writing it!

76.

Recruiting Mentors

When you ask a question one of three things happens. The person you ask doesn't answer or doesn't know the answer. The person gives you the answer. The person is so intrigued by the question, that they tell you to call them the next time you have a question. And suddenly, you have a mentor.

We were very blessed with our laws. The idea of the Next of Kin bills struck such a deep emotional cord, that many people we called for advice, told us to count on them any time we needed input. And since we were dealing with an area and people we had absolutely no experience with, we took them up on the offer!

Have you ever wondered how successful people seem to become more and more successful in every area of their lives? They recruit mentors! I bet most of them don't even realize that they're doing it. Actors do it all the time. Let's say they're in a TV series like *Grey's Anatomy* and they decide that they'd really like a director's credit on their resume. So they wander around the set one day, stand behind the director and look over his shoulder. As any self-respecting director would do, he or she will ask the actor what the heck they're doing. "Oh nothing," they'll say, "just wondering what life looks like from this side of the camera." Before you know it, they'll be sitting on the camera, discussing camera angles and lighting and sure enough next season, that actor will be directing an episode!

If you don't want to end up reinventing the wheel, mentors are absolutely crucial to your eventual success in your new job or undertaking. Sometimes it's easy. You talk to someone to ask a question or for a piece of advice and you just hit it off.

Other times, you need to recruit your mentor. This is true in any are of your life – finances, having a better marriage, anything -- not just your career. The key is to find a person or people who have expertise in the area you need. If you want to learn how to invest, find a person who is phenomenal at investing. If you want to become a better accountant, or writer, or salesperson, call around, do some research, find two or three of the absolutely best accountants, writers or salespersons you can and approach them, either by letter or phone call as we outlined in the section on Advice Calls.

For the first meeting or phone call, stick to a few specific questions and try not to take up a lot of their time. If you like the feedback you're getting, seem to get along well and they leave the door open for further contact, then be sure to contact them the next time you have a question.

Always be brief, polite and remember to send a short thank you note after that first meeting. Even an email can really brighten someone's day.

If the relationship begins to grow, then sit down with this person and tell them that you've been looking for a mentor in their area of expertise.

Let them know what your goals are, how you plan to achieve them and ask them if they would be willing to meet with you (again email is great for this) on a regular basis for advice and feedback. If they can't do it themselves, ask them to recommend a few other people who you can contact.

And, although the advice won't be quite as personalized, don't forget that there is a wealth of information in books. We're so blessed in this world to be able to get the input of people like Sir John Templeton for financial advice, Richard Branson and Michael Eisner for advice on building a company and countless other experts, just by walking into a library or a bookstore.

Building An Advisory Board

Very often, a relationship that begins as an advice call and turns into mentorship, will go even farther. Suddenly the venture that you're involved in or the business you're growing will become so worthwhile or valuable, that the people who have been advising you will want to become involved in it. This is exactly what happened to us with the bills. The associations, lobby groups and experts who mentored us about the legislative process, ended up lobbying for or acting as experts on the bills themselves. Before we knew it, we had an informal board of advisors, who had an actual stake in the subject in which they were advising us.

Now not only do we have an entire group of experts to talk to when something unfamiliar comes up, we also have a group to go to when something interesting happens. For example, we've decided to add an app to our Call My Family hospital training program. One e-mail to the gang telling them about what we're going to be doing and they're emailing us back with advice, contacts and asking to be involved in the program in any way they can. This is an incredibly powerful way to be proactive!

Just promise us one thing. When you get to be an expert in your new field, don't forget to return the favor and make yourself available to up-and-comers looking for their own mentors. And don't forget to do everything you can to give back to the people who helped you. Every time we find an article we think will be of interest to them, or people that they should meet or even jobs or board positions they might want to pursue, we contact them ASAP. Remember, one of the most powerful laws of the universe – Give and it shall be given unto you.

Chapter Thirteen

WHAT IF?

What If...

You still haven't found the perfect career?

If, at this point you still don't know exactly what career path to follow, we have a few suggestions that might help.

First, go back and read over the answers you gave to the exercises in the book. Be absolutely honest with yourself. Are the answers you gave the ones you think you should give or do they truly reflect your real feelings? It's so easy to fall into the trap of thinking that a certain profession is the way to go, just because we've gotten it into our heads that it will bring in a lot of money or that it's what our family or friends think we should be doing. There is only one expert on your career path or mission in life and that person is YOU! After all, you're the one who's going to have to live with whatever decision you make and put in the hours doing the job.

Another thing to keep in mind is that as uncomfortable as it might be, you may have to start thinking out of the box. People have a tendency to think that they only way they're going to get a job in a different area, is to have specific experience in it.

As you've seen in the book, that's simply no longer the case. The world is changing so quickly that most employers are looking for people who can think on their feet and who can bring a great skill mix to the company, in many areas, and not necessarily the one they're being hired for. So keep an open mind and as you look at these exercises or redo them, give your heart a chance to chime in before you write your responses.

Chapter Fourteen

BUILDING YOUR LIFE

Building Your Life

You've come to another plateau. You've found out a lot about your personality, your dreams and your ambitions. The purpose of your life has begun to come to light and you've learned how to stop dreaming about it and make it a reality. You have even begun those first steps to your new career. Since we spend about sixty percent of our lives working, it only makes sense that we spend that time doing something we love.

But what about the other forty percent of your life? Why work hard all day to come home to a boring life, or make great money if you have to work until midnight every night and have no time to enjoy it.

The point we're trying to make is, you need a balanced life. If you let yourself get burned out, you won't be good for anything. And that certainly won't help you perform your life's purpose.

Very few people who reach the end of their lives ever regret something they have done; they always regret what they haven't done. Give yourself the greatest gift of all. Don't put off living. Make time for that special weekend you and your spouse have always planned, or the piano lessons you promised yourself. We instinctively tell ourselves what we need. That's why personal goals are just as important as career goals.

EXERCISE 8

To find your personal goals, first, make a list of everything you absolutely must do or experience in your lifetime. What can't you imagine not doing before you leave the earth?

Second, read over all your answers to the exercises. However wonderful your main career is, there's no way that it will let you pursue every interest you have. All those other things you enjoy, might make a great home business, long term project, hobby or even an opportunity for you to teach or write books that might inspire a whole new generation of career seekers on their own path.

The trick of building an exciting well-rounded life, is to figure out what is important to you and fit it into your life. When the puzzle finally fits together it will be a beautiful mosaic of a rich full life.

And what more can anyone ask for?

APPENDIX

Here are some other great books to read on this subject.

Bolles, Richard What Color Is Your Parachute? Ten Speed Press 2016
http://amzn.to/1TLxKtO

Anderson, Nancy <u>Work With Passion: How To Do What You Love For A Living</u>
New World Library 2012 http://amzn.to/1XFmLaX

Sinetar, Marsha <u>Do What You Love, The Money Will Follow</u> Dell Books 1989
http://amzn.to/1W6SmTr

We'd love to hear from you, with your comments and success stories.

If you'd like to order extra copies of *Get Paid To Do What You Love* for yourself, your friends, or your family, you can find them on Amazon.com or at our website www.getyourstufftogether.com

Want to order *Get Paid To Do What You Love* in bulk for businesses, groups or organizations? E-mail us at corpsales@getyourstufftogether.com for **special pricing.**

Come visit The Backup Plan Blog for quick and easy ways to safeguard your home, your keepsakes and the people you love, from life's little and not so little emergencies.

Go to: http://rnn10.wordpress.com

―――――

Want To Follow The Backup Plan?

Go to: https://rnn10.wordpress.com/media-resources/

―――――

For Other Books By Janet Greenwald & Laura Greenwald, Including:

Get Your Stuff Together
The Backup Plan 3.0
Take This Book To Your Parent's House
The ICE My Phone Kit
& The Wealth of Tulips

Go to: www.getyourstufftogether.com

Customization and Bulk Discounts Available

About The Authors

Janet and Laura are one of the only mother/daughter writing teams in the entertainment industry. They began their careers in production on network sitcoms at MGM and Warner Bros and are currently developing their own original movies and television series through their production company Lion And The Rock Entertainment.

The Greenwalds were introduced to emergency preparedness the hard way, when a jumbo-jet crashed across the street from their home. But it was a horrendous medical tragedy – one that took the life of their mother/grandmother, Elaine Sullivan – that propelled them into new territory.

When Elaine's hospital failed to notify Jan and Laura of her hospitalization they were not only prevented from being at her side, but they were also kept from preventing the drug interaction that took Elaine's life.

After uncovering a loophole in the laws which regulate the notification of the next of kin of hospital patients, Laura & Jan joined forces with legislators in Illinois and California to enact three Next of Kin Laws, before creating Notify In 7, a training program that provides hospital professionals with the skills they need to notify and reunite trauma victims with their loved ones, quickly and easily, as well as the upcoming Call My Family App. Hoping to keep other families from experiencing the same thing they had, they turned their story into a screenplay called Without Consent, now in development as a feature film.

Their latest book The Backup Plan 3.0, gives readers quick and easy steps they can take to keep everything that's important to them organized, safe, sound and accessible. Each section – over 30 in all – covers a different area from backing up and fixing family photos, home movies and music, to creating an evacuation plan, securing vital documents, medical information, financial information and data.

Between their books, blog and website, over 370,000 people have used Jan and Laura's shortcut sheets, action plans and materials to keep themselves, their homes, their families and the things that they love, safe and secure.